TOM HENRICKSEN

Agile Basics in 60 Minutes - 2nd Edition

Contents

Preface

It has been a few years since I published the original. I thought it was time to update and expand this work. Many things have changed since then. Of course, the core principles remain.

As you start your journey this will help you understand the basics. You can get started quickly and make progress. Remember the most important piece is to keep moving forward. You will make mistakes and that is okay.

I have organized this to make it more approachable. Each part contains a specific section that you will need. Read and then come back to it as you have questions.

I

Part One

In this first part, we cover some basics about why the agile movement came about. Then we discuss the origins of Scrum and where Agile is today. Finally, we cover some benefits.

1

Why Are Changes Needed? Failings of the Old Way

Photo by Florian Klauer on Unsplash

Software development has had some historically monumental failures. In 2011, a financial services giant had a software glitch that cost investors $217 million, which resulted in a $25 million fine from the U.S. Securities and Exchange Commission.

The typical waterfall process has produced many scary disasters that make headlines like this. The traditional method of gathering requirements, designing, coding the solution, integrating the pieces, and testing at the end has many drawbacks, including:

- Its simple, linear, and structured approach;
- A great amount of time spent in the requirements and design phases to reduce the cost of coding and testing;
- Being more disciplined in its procedure, translates into less flexibility in the entire development process.

Additionally, the requirements are not understood. Before I worked on Agile projects, I would cringe when I heard, "I think we want to change this." Or, "We already talked about that."

The users often don't know what they want until they see the first output (page layout or even simple calculation functionality) of your software. Even with mock-ups or wireframes, we have a hard time zeroing in on what the customer may want.

2

Agile Manifesto

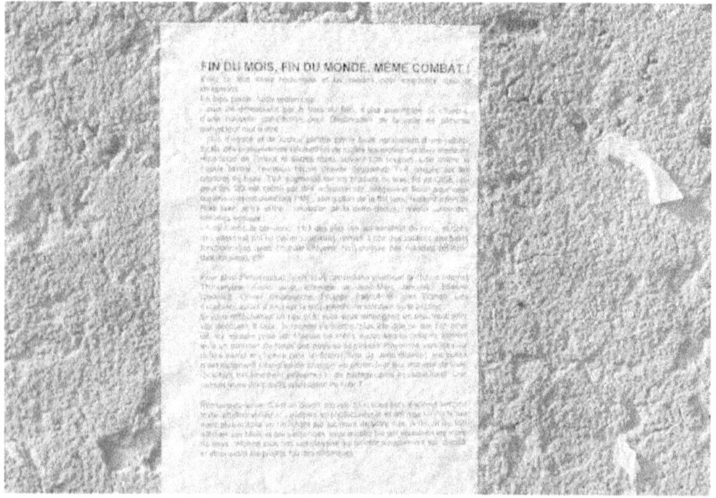

Photo by ev on Unsplash

In 2001 a group of software development leaders got together
and created a declaration of their views on software develop-

ment that specifically outlined the changes they wanted to lead. This is called the Agile Manifesto. It states the values they want to advance:

1. Individuals and interactions over processes and tools
2. Working software over comprehensive documentation
3. Customer collaboration over contract negotiation
4. Responding to change over following a plan

The key is to make the process lightweight and adaptive to change. They want to remove strict processes that we sometimes use to construct software and collaborate with customers to produce working software.

It's about welcoming change and embracing it as part of the iterative process to get what we (the software development team AND customers) want.

In working on a healthcare job site, we would try to get the priorities for the upcoming year. We would complete a project, ask for feedback, and would end up missing the mark many times.

When we switched to Agile, we had many more opportunities for feedback built in and we were able to better achieve customers' objectives. The iterative nature of Agile development facilitates feedback at numerous points through the development process.

Agile asks us to have frequent check-ins with stakeholders. The daily Scrum meeting is where the team checks in with each other on progress in the current Sprint; the Retro is a look back to identify what did we right and what can we improve on.

In traditional waterfall projects, we might work six months or a year before doing something like this. An Agile discipline demands collaboration and communication that will result in efficiency and quality.

3

Scrum Origins

Photo by Giu Vicente on Unsplash

Scrum was born out of work on eXtreme programming when Kent Beck collaborated with Jeff Sutherland. The term "scrum" itself was used as the result of a paper in the *Harvard Business Review*. Takeuchi and Nonaka wrote "The New New Product Development Game" in 1986 while working with many multinational companies in Japan and the United States.

In today's fast-paced, fiercely competitive world of commercial new product development, speed and flexibility are essential. Companies are increasingly realizing that the old, sequential approach to developing new products simply won't get the job done. Instead, companies in Japan and the United States are using a holistic method—as in rugby, the ball gets passed within the team as it moves as a unit up the field.

—Hirotaka Takeuchi and Ikujiro Nonaka, "The New New Product Development Game"

The paper details the aspects of the old sequential way of product development (i.e., waterfall), similar to the traditional software development model where there are discrete stages in the process. The new design process is overlapping work where a multidisciplinary team works together.

This can be a big change for engineers and quality assurance people working together back and forth to complete a feature, or a Product Owner working hand in hand with a web designer to hash out a page layout. This can make things move faster, versus having numerous meetings over days and weeks to come to a consensus.

Mike Beedle and Ken Schwaber worked together to codify some of the basic tenets of Scrum while working at Individual Inc. They joined forces to write the book *Agile Software Development with Scrum.*

They guided Individual Inc. through learning the Scrum methodology. First, they started out getting a prioritized list of requirements to build the product backlog. They started a

month-long Sprint, releasing code to production at the end of
that month. The team had not been released in the nine months
before that.

4

Is Agile Dead?

Photo by Ross Findon on Unsplash

Since this was originally published ten years ago agile has gone through an evolution. The popularity has waned a bit. Any change experiences backlash. This prompted people to state Agile is dead.

From my vantage point it is not dead it has just been accepted. Teams generally use agile practices like Scrum. They may have modified things a bit. Overall it is there.

Of course, it is important to point out that agile is no panacea. It doesn't solve problems as much as it reveals them. Organizations might avoid using the techniques but they will slowly fade away.

5

The Benefits of Agile

Photo by Towfiqu barbhuiya on Unsplash

Agile emphasizes short cycles or iterations of work, with continuous feedback to zero in on what the customer wants quickly and deliver value. There is also continuous planning, testing, and integration to keep the product evolving to meet business goals.

Agile is also lightweight and adaptable when compared to traditional waterfall software development. There is a shift to empower team members to collaborate and make decisions quickly.

- Product Owner prioritizes the backlog
- Sprint duration is fixed (usually two weeks)
- Shippable software at the end of each Sprint
- Sprint ends with a demo of work and a retrospective with the team
- Team chooses work from the backlog for the next Sprint

The team is always working on the highest-value items as designated by the Product Owner. Scrum strives to deliver the maximum value in the shortest time. Change is embraced in the stories within the product backlog; once it is accepted into a Sprint, there can be no changes in the user story.

II

Part Two

Here we cover the basics of Scrum. At its core it is quite simple. The best way to learn it is to try it out.

6

The Basic Foundation

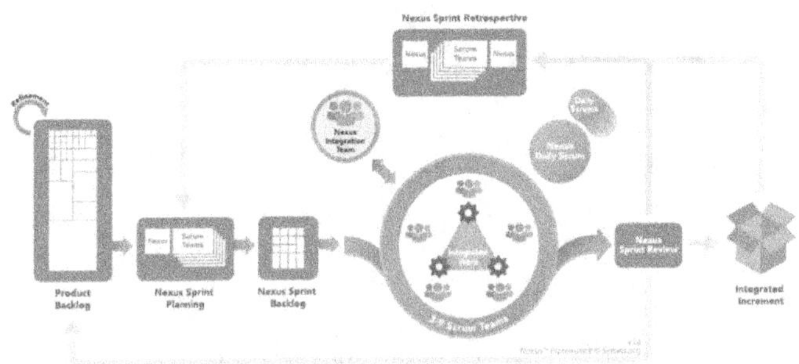

Scrum is one of many Agile processes. *Scrum is an Agile process that allows us to focus on delivering the highest business value in the shortest time.* It allows us to rapidly and repeatedly inspect actual working software (every two weeks to one month).

The main notion is to get some enhancement out to users and iterate over changes to determine if we are giving our clients value. The business, via the Product Owner, sets the priorities for the Agile team.

The Agile Team will self-organize to determine the best way to deliver the highest-priority features. This doesn't mean that people can do whatever they want; they have to collectively agree on things like team norms, what is acceptable, and what is not acceptable.

This can require some give and take between the business and the Agile team, and between Agile team members. As points are given to enhancements, the team should only commit to its average velocity.

Every two weeks to a month, anyone can see the real working software and decide to release it as-is or continue to enhance it for another Sprint. By breaking up features and getting them out sooner, we provide real business value.

7

Scrum Roles

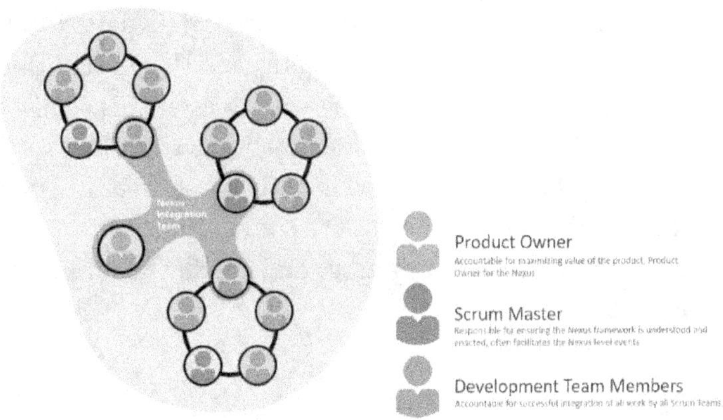

A Scrum team has three main roles that make up the team. We will discuss each role that the team has and the tasks they are responsible for. Also, we will discuss how the team works with those outside of the main team.

Product Owner

The Product Owner brings the business requirements to the team. They are responsible for the product and creating a vision for it. *They work with the stakeholders and end users to gather requirements.*

They use the demands of various stakeholders to build and prioritize the product backlog and create a release plan. The Product Owner is tasked with creating clear requirements and acceptance criteria.

Scrum Master

The Scrum Master is the team coach and leads the team through the Sprint. They facilitate all team meetings and foster a trusting and collaborative environment. The Scrum Master will negotiate with the Product Owner on how to meet business goals.

They must keep things moving forward and remove any obstacles to the team's progress in a Sprint. The Scrum Master leads all Scrum-related processes and coaches the business about all things Scrum.

Team

The team estimates their stories makes their designs and implements them. The team is made of many different disciplines; programmers, designers, testers, and perhaps DBAs or administrators are some of the roles that could be on a Scrum team.

The team has quite a bit of autonomy and can chart their course. The team commits to delivering the software at consistent increments (usually two- to four-week Sprints) for the

Product Owner and business.

Others (Pigs and Chickens)

Agile addresses other parties and stakeholders as chickens: in the famous line about bacon and eggs, the chicken is involved but the pig is committed. Mike Cohn, an Agile leader, refers to the team in Agile as "having their bacon on the line."

The team, Product Owner, and Scrum Master are all pigs in this scenario. A chicken is someone who is gaining from the pig's work and performance. Other stakeholders and interested parties are chickens and this gives them less input in the operation.

8

The Sprint

Photo by Parabol | The Agile Meeting Tool on Unsplash

The Agile process breaks down work into something called a Sprint. The Sprint length can be as short as two weeks or as long as four weeks. This is just a recommendation that I have seen.

I have heard of companies doing one-week and even one-day Sprints. Progress occurs in a series of legs. Small features will be completed in one Sprint, while larger features will be finished over multiple Sprints.

To release software to a production environment is something that we struggled with when I worked at Dice. Do you need to release after every Sprint? This depends if your code is ready.

Sometimes you may have large features that may take a few Sprints to complete. The product or feature is designed, then coded and tested during the Sprint.

To accomplish this, you need to break down projects into workable chunks, or tasks, in your Sprint cycle. This is where the normal six-month objectives must be divided up.

At Dice, before our Agile changeover, we had six-month objectives that were large and would change. Getting people to focus on what was the highest priority for the next Sprint proved challenging.

Once you determine your items for the next Sprint, you must lock in on those and **not change them during the Sprint**. If you start changing your items during the Sprint cycle, you could get into some "thrashing" where little is accomplished but causes frustration to the team.

9

Daily Scrum or Standup

Photo by Jason Goodman on Unsplash

One of the most helpful practices in Scrum is the Daily Standup Meeting or Daily Scrum. The team gathers around the scrum board and updates their Sprint status by providing the answers to the following three questions:

1. What did you do yesterday?
2. What will you do today?
3. Is there anything in your way?

The role of this meeting is not simply to give status updates to your Scrum Master or project manager, it is to commit to action on the tasks you will do today as well as to alert the team of any roadblocks.

By announcing to your teammates what you are working on that day, you show what you are planning to do. This is a good time for other developers to offer help to you.

The Scrum, or simply the Standup, is purposely intended to be kept under fifteen minutes. I was working with another team on their Agile transformation and they would always sit down. This simple act of sitting down made the meetings drag out.

A conversation of commitments always got sidetracked into what problems they had been having from the last release. The job of the Scrum Master is to keep these meetings moving. If someone has a "blocker," the Scrum Master's job is to remove the issue(s) that are in their way.

Ideally, this doesn't happen in a conference or meeting room as this will usually lead to longer meetings. It should be held every day at the same time and place to build continuity. The whole idea of the daily scrum doesn't sound that groundbreaking, but it can help your team create great results.

10

Sprint Demo

Photo by Austin Distel on Unsplash

The Sprint demo is a chance to show what has been completed during the Sprint. In each Sprint we want to have potentially shippable software, therefore this is the place where we come to show our accomplishments. There is a demonstration of new features and enhancements that the Product Owner deemed the highest priority.

The people invited to a Sprint demo are a long list: we show management and other external stakeholders or customers as well as the Product Owner, Scrum Master, and the team. The team is measured against the goals set out during the Sprint planning meeting.

11

Sprint Retro

One of the most important pieces of Agile is the Sprint retro. This is a time to do some examination of the practices and see where you may be succeeding and failing. We have all heard it before but there always is room for improvement.

This is usually the last meeting of a Sprint. The meeting should take approximately one hour and include the Product Owner, the Scrum Master, and the team.

One activity that can be done in a Sprint retro is called Start, Stop, and Continue. We begin by giving everyone on the core team three sticky notes. We ask them to write three things down, one for each sticky note. They can choose from the following:

Something we should **START** doing.

Something we should **STOP** doing.

Something we should **CONTINUE** doing.

They can write one from each or all from one area, it doesn't matter. Once complete, the team members add them to the whiteboard and read them aloud to the group. After everyone is done, we give everyone three votes or dots with a marker to vote.

Then we take the top items and see if we can make option items for our next Sprint. We had two items that we took for action items in our next Sprint. Here are some more retro ideas.

12

Sprint Planning

The next step for the Agile team is to have a Sprint planning meeting. The outcome of this meeting should be a prioritized list of items or a Sprint backlog. This Sprint backlog has the user stories ranked in their order of importance.

Since we have already estimated the items in our backlog grooming, we know roughly how hard the features are. This planning process will take some time to get the whole team to agree on what can be accomplished during the Sprint. The Scrum Master will facilitate this meeting, and the Product Owner should be available to answer user stories or priority questions.

Your initial sprints can be hectic. The team will struggle a bit. As you gain experience things will get better. For instance, if you forget to look at people's vacations you might have some stories flounder. Learn as you go. Be patient as it takes time for the team to change and adapt.

The condition of the product backlog has a direct impact on your ability to plan the Sprint. If it is not constantly groomed, then your Sprint planning loses its impact. Also, the business conditions may have an impact too. If the business is under a constant state of change it can be hard to plan the Sprint and complete the tasks.

When you plan a Sprint, you need to realistically understand any technological constraints that may hinder the project completion. There may be a few items that the business asked for and we had to allow time for exploration of new technologies to see how we could implement a solution. These tasks are hard to estimate and may involve a technology spike.

13

Sprint Backlog

The stories the team has agreed to work on during the Sprint is called the Sprint backlog. These user stories are selected from the product backlog, therefore these items have been reviewed for proper format, estimated, and prioritized by the Product Owner. The team has committed to completing all the stories in the Sprint backlog during the Sprint.

The team will create the Sprint backlog during the Sprint planning meeting. They will usually take the highest priority items in the product backlog depending on the estimate and the team's Sprint velocity. The team selects the stories to add to the Sprint backlog, not the Product Owner.

The developers should always start by picking the highest-priority user story off the Sprint backlog when getting something new for development. It is important to complete the highest-priority items first so that if something happens to slip, it is a lower-priority user story.

The Sprint backlog is to be updated daily as to each user story's progress. It can be done during the daily standup meeting. This can help teammates track progress on items and see if any help is needed to get something wrapped up. If there are roadblocks to progress, the Scrum Master should step in and remove them.

When creating the Sprint backlog it is important to look at each team member's strengths and not try to overload one team member. The Sprint backlog does not assign tasks to team members; as developers' schedules become free, they pick the highest-priority user story. Also, each developer should limit their **work in progress** to one story at a time.

III

Part Three

Here we dive into user stories and their parts. Plus I share some typical struggles you may encounter.

14

User Stories

User stories are nice, informal ways to share requirements for software development. While I was working at IFMC (now Telligen), we went through a process to get to CMMI Level 1. In the process, we started gathering extensive requirement documents. I felt bad for the business analyst who put them together as no one read them. User stories are neither lengthy nor vague like some requirements documents.

User stories are short, simple descriptions of a feature told from the perspective of the person who desires the new functionality, usually a user or customer of the system. —Mike Cohn, Mountain Goat Software

User stories should be short and right to the point. They simply try to gather the most important information, or as Joe Friday would say in *Dragnet*, "Just the facts, ma'am." We want to capture the who, the what, and the why of the requested feature or enhancement. The best way to capture a user story is simply to write it down on a note card or sticky note and add this to the product backlog.

The form of a user story usually fits the basic template:

As a <role>, I want <feature/enhancement> so that <benefit>.

For example, "As a driver, I want a radio so that I can be entertained while driving." User stories should also include some acceptance criteria, or definitions or indications of what "done" is. The acceptance criteria should address what needs to be tested.

The user story won't always be complete. It may need some additional refinement and is created to start the conversation between the business and development. Anyone can create a user story: developers, testers, and/or Product Owners. The Product Owner should review all user stories to make sure they have the proper information.

15

Acceptance Criteria

A key component of the user story is the acceptance criteria.

Acceptance criteria define the boundaries of a user story and are used to confirm when a story is completed and working as intended.

When we add in the acceptance criteria, we spell out specifics that fulfill the requirements. This removes any ambiguity in the story that the developer may see. The criteria come from asking the Product Owner a few questions about what makes the story "done." We all make assumptions and that can get tricky as everyone has a different frame of reference.

A user story example

As a job seeker, I want to log in so I can post my resume.

The user story gives us some information about the particular feature, but it seems there might be some additional details we want to address before we start coding. When we say "post a resume," what do we mean? Just upload the file? Or do we manually enter previous job experience?

Acceptance criteria can be gained by having a conversation with the Product Owner, the developer, and the quality assurance team member.

Sometimes these questions will come up in an estimation meeting; this will help everyone agree on what is to be done. The acceptance criteria should be spelled out in simple language and avoid the use of excessive business jargon. The acceptance criteria will serve as the minimum product requirements.

Example Acceptance Criteria:

1. The login button needs to be blue and say "Login."
2. The password field needs to allow up to twelve characters.
3. The password must contain one number, one letter, and one special character.

Once the developer has completed their work, they can hand it over to quality assurance. Then quality assurance can test the new feature thoroughly with the criteria in mind.

16

Story Points

Photo by Buddha Elemental 3D on Unsplash

Story points are a simple unit of measure for a software development team. They are completely arbitrary and will vary from team to team. *Story points are not correlated to hours of completion.* The points are an abstract measure of the complexity of the user story.

Story points are sometimes measured in the **Fibonacci sequence of 1,2,3,5,8,13,21,34,45**... Some will measure in T-shirt sizes S, M, L, and XL. I have even heard an interesting idea of using dog breeds as a sizing measure. To get things started, you discuss with the team a baseline user story of making a small change (as an example).

Then, you talk through what each team member thinks; the estimate should try to come to a consensus. *It is important to point out again that given two different teams, they will come to different story point totals.*

We estimate user stories in our product backlog to look at the complexity of a user story. This also helps the Product Owner compare different user stories as they prioritize items for an upcoming Sprint.

Also, as a team goes through a few Sprints and gets a consistent cadence, we can use the story points to help estimate how much work can be completed in a period.

When you are estimating a user story in a product backlog you will see great differences in each person's estimate. This will lead to a good discussion on why someone might have a one and somebody else has an eight. Trends will emerge as you work with your team and you will learn people's approaches and personalities.

Remember, points are a measurement of the amount of work that could be completed in a given Sprint. As the team becomes used to estimating, team members will become more comfortable – and more efficient – with this part of the process.

After all this, we also have people that don't like story points. They can be misused and create some waste. This article covers whether you should or should not estimate.

17

User Story Struggles

User stories can be challenging to get right. I remember struggling with them the first time I worked on a Scrum team. I fall into the camp of too little detail. In my waterfall days before that, I would rarely have read the business requirements.

Things were always in a state of flux so clear requirements were much like the Loch Ness monster. You heard stories of them but, never saw them. Let' go over a few common struggles people run into.

Started to early

Stories occasionally get pulled into the sprint that was not quite ready. I am eager to get work done. As a scrum master, I would overlook some of the missing information. My team did a good job of learning this.

They would review the items and see if something was missing. Try to develop a checklist that helps guide whether you have all the information. I have seen many teams do this and each checklist is a little different.

Start easy tasks

Sometimes developers start easy tasks first and never get to the more challenging tasks till later in the sprint. One thing I tried to do was have the easy tasks left until later in the sprint to fill time later.

Start the hardest ones first and give yourself the most time on those. After a while, the team will get used to this and jump on the harder tasks right away.

Size Matters

I remember in college I took some economics classes. The professors always would talk about widget production. This fictional item of production threw me for a loop. I like to visualize things. A widget is hard to imagine.

Economics was not of much interest to me, so my imagination would wander. When teams start to look at the size of user stories it can be hard to determine if it is an epic or user story. Or what part can we complete in the sprint?

Work Left

Mike Cohn from Mountain Goat Software says, "Ideally, a team would finish every item on its sprint backlog every sprint. But, for a variety of reasons, that isn't always the case." He reminds us to re-examine the work left and check to see if it is still important. Perhaps we may need to split some of the user stories up. I am glad Mike reminds us to look for the root cause. Each team is different and we need to learn from our mistakes.

Lifecycle

There are many stages to the user story life cycle. In this post, they break it down into fives stages. The first stage is "Not Started" when it comes out of the sprint planning. Then once we begin to work on it, the story is "In Progress".

The team completes the work and it becomes, "Done." Depending on the approval of the user story it can be "Accepted" or "Rejected." Occasionally stories will get "Cancelled" as they are no longer relevant. These are not hard and fast rules so your team could create their statuses.

Tips

Roman Pichler is a big name in the agile world. He shares some great tips here. He reminds us that the user comes first. So keep the customer or user perspective on top of your mind. Create the stories collaboratively. Just as it points out in the Agile Manifesto, "Individuals and interactions over processes and tools."

Refine the story until it is ready to go. Rarely does something start ready it takes some time to sort out. His last point reminds us not to just use user stories. There are many other things to try along with maps, diagrams, storyboards, and more.

Something Smells

Occasionally people do something that feels a bit icky. Like taking some old waterfall requirements document and shoehorning it into a user story. People try to keep their waterfall habits in an agile world.

Perhaps it is an acceptance criteria list that looks a little too long. Agile is founded on conversations and many of these novel-like documents are a conversation avoidance technique. If something smells in your user story make sure and take out the trash!

IV

Part Four

These are some additional items you will need to know. For instance, a good team starts with Working Agreements. Plus a few helpful items with backlogs.

18

Grooming and Estimation

Photo by benjamin lehman on Unsplash

Now that you have created a product backlog, we need to take the next step and groom and estimate the items in it. This is what happens in a backlog grooming meeting. We bring together the scrum team and the Scrum Master will lead this meeting with lots of questions for the Product Owner.

We begin to clarify requirements and user stories, we try to ask questions that tease out requirements and enhance the user stories so a developer can estimate. Another important item to add to the user stories is acceptance criteria.

These first help the developer know what needs to be added as well as let the tester know what to look for. I find adding these gets everyone thinking on the same page about what is being asked for.

If we have enough information, we can estimate the development time or size of the request. When we first started doing estimates, we used hour estimates. We had Agile consultants come in and they recommended against that.

They said, "How this can be used by outside parties to gauge how much work it takes?" They thought it was better to just use the Fibonacci sequence or T-shirt sizes. We started with the Fibonacci sequence and it worked pretty well for us.

Occasionally we come to a request that is large in a backlog grooming meeting. As mentioned earlier, we call these large items epics. These need to be broken down into separate items that can be added to upcoming Sprints.

It is best to schedule a separate meeting to discuss these large items. There might be a need for additional research to determine all the pieces involved. This additional scope can be worked on in a meeting called a "three amigos" meeting.

The backlog grooming meeting precedes the Sprint planning meeting. We will talk about that next. A Sprint planning meeting is getting us ready for our first Sprint.

19

Product Backlog

How do you know what needs to be completed unless you start with a list? A product backlog is a list of features and changes to be done. The product backlog list must be ordered in the priority they should be completed.

Usually, the business owner and scrum team will meet to list out all these items and build the product backlog. Having a good product backlog will help you get your work ready for the first Sprint or the next Sprint. Each item needs to be clearly defined and we need to understand what systems will be touched and who will complete the work.

You also need to discuss the why. "Why do we need this?" This can help you work on prioritization. Some tasks may have preliminary items that need to be completed. Outside dependencies can be a big issue.

When I was at Scrum Master training, I spoke to a few people from Nationwide Insurance. They have Agile teams dependent on non-Agile teams that may have a six-month lead time, so you need to get your request in early. Each item needs the requirements or user story of what the completed feature will do.

Working at Dice, our first foray into Agile was cut short by not having a well-defined product backlog. The team worked hard to capture the items the business owners wanted. The problem they ran into was getting the right people involved.

When I was in sales they always told me to "talk to the decision-maker." They ran into an issue where at Dice, they had too many decision-makers as well as some people who would not get involved. The product backlog lacked some key items.

20

Backlog Grooming

The Agile team periodically will meet to groom the backlog. Grooming involves reviewing user stories to check for their completeness. As a Scrum Master, I would ask, "Is there enough information to estimate?"

Perhaps we need to get some questions answered by the Product Owner. Also, some stories might not be relevant anymore and could be removed from the backlog. This meeting is attended by the team, Product Owner, and Scrum Master.

The Product Owner can update the team on the priority changes to the backlog if there are any. The user stories that are complete can be estimated with story points. Stories that have been estimated are eligible to be planned into a Sprint. Some previously estimated stories may need to be re-estimated if there is new information or changes in the story.

During the Sprint, a previously estimated story may be more complex than we originally thought. In this situation, we might have to split a user story into multiple stories and then estimate these new stories in the backlog grooming meeting. Sometimes we may estimate a user story that turns out to be more of an epic and needs to be broken down further.

21

Epics

Photo by Kalen Emsley on Unsplash

Sometimes you run into a large user story that needs to be broken apart. In Agile we call those "epics." There are no hard and fast rules on what is an epic, or even what is a user story.

Primarily, though, one way to break them down is that a user story is completed in one Sprint. If it requires more than a Sprint's worth of work, it is probably an epic.

An epic captures a large body of work. It is essentially a large user story that can be broken down into several smaller stories. It may take several Sprints to complete an epic.

—via Atlassian

An example of an epic would be, "Implement a Single Sign On service to all production applications." This would take a lot of time to implement and involve different parts of the organization.

Epics will require coordination of various business units and numerous releases, ergo multiple Sprints. Sometimes they will involve business partners or other companies.

In researching this, I liked how the Scaled Agile Framework calls out the distinction between business and architecture epics. The business epic is a large initiative for the internal business or business partners.

An example of a business epic would be, "Create a new accounting reporting system." An architecture epic is a large change in the underlying technology to support current or future business needs.

An example architecture epic would be, "Upgrade application servers to Node.js 20." In my experience, a new business epic could require one or many architecture epics.

22

Working Agreements and Definition of Done

Photo by Austin Distel on Unsplash

Agile teams need to come up with a working agreement or "team norms" to help set the ground rules. This is a good exercise to do early in the Agile transformation. The team needs to figure out how it can handle some of the critical questions it will see in the Sprints.

How to address bugs or fires that come up during a Sprint. We want to avoid changes that come up during a Sprint but, things happen. Do we want to designate someone to handle these things? Try not to make one person do this all the time; rotate this responsibility.

The use of information radiators, planning boards, and Sprint boards. The group needs to come up with guidelines for what information radiators to use and who uses them.

Primarily the Product Owner is responsible for keeping the planning board up to date and prioritized. This is important when Sprint planning is starting. The team can then update the Sprint board as they complete development and complete testing.

The **definition of done** is a big topic to decide as well. Developers may think a project is done when it works on their machine in Chrome, but quality assurance will want to check it in other browsers and pass an automated regression too. The Product Owner might want to review it as well. Each group has its definition.

23

Definition of Ready

Photo by Asher Legg on Unsplash

In Agile development, a **user story is pulled into a Sprint when it is ready, and a team needs to have a definition of ready**. Before I spoke about working agreements and the definition of done.

Today, we need to discuss the importance of having a definition of ready. The team needs to set up the rules so the Product Owner can put things in the proper format.

The most popular format for the user story is from Mike Cohn: *As a <type of user>, I want <some goal> so that <some reason>.* We also want acceptance criteria added to the user story.

These two things helped us get the user story thought through. Without this basic information, we would be guessing.

This gives us the benefit of having clearly defined work that can help us avoid expensive rework. It gives us the ability to push back when we see vague or incomplete information. Once we had these two items completed, we would review them at our backlog grooming meeting and estimate the item.

According to Agile leader Roman Pilcher, "A 'ready' item should be clear, feasible, and testable." He defines a user story as being clear if all team members understand its definition. He suggests working collaboratively to create the user story and add the acceptance criteria.

Roman defines feasible work as work able to be completed in one Sprint. Testable stories have a simple way to determine whether the functionality is complete.

The Product Owner must be aware of the definition of ready. The Scrum Master is tasked with helping enforce these standards so the team can only get work when it is well defined. Other items to be called out can be dependencies for this item, any applicable performance criteria, and the person who can accept the story.

24

Information Radiators

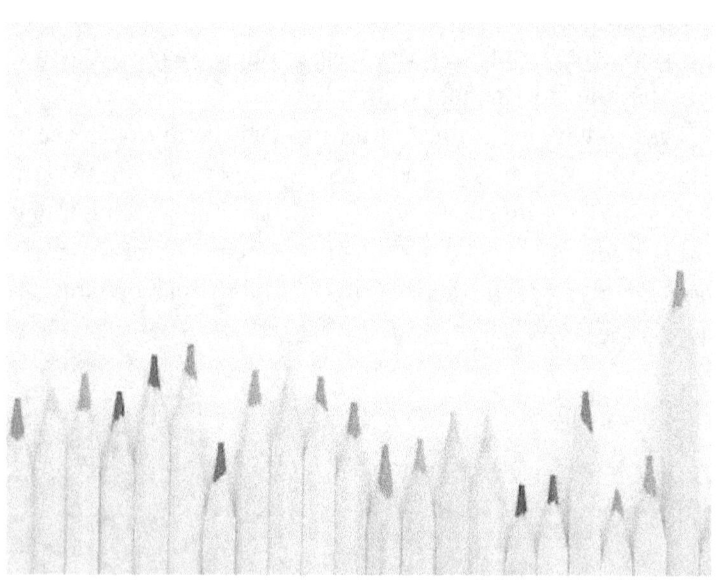

Photo by Jess Bailey on Unsplash

In Agile we use information radiators to convey data quickly and easily. They are put in a highly visible spot and communicate the team's progress on each Sprint. The term was coined by Alistair Cockburn.

These radiators are used to convey information to others not on the team as well. The idea is for management and other departments to walk by and see the information and quickly understand where the team is at. They are updated constantly to communicate the current status.

Sprint Board

The Sprint board is the list of tasks for the current Sprint; some call it a task board. Usually, you will have columns denoting where in the completion cycle the work is. This board must get updated every day, perhaps during the morning scrum or standup meeting. This board is great at showing the team's real-time progress on the current work in the Sprint. As outsiders walk by this, they should be able to quickly see the progress.

For instance, you may have a "to-do" column for items not yet started. Then you might have an "in progress" or "doing" column to put items of the Sprint currently being worked on. The next column could be your last column, "done" or "code complete" for development that is done; next it may move to test. The beauty of Agile, and in some people's eyes, the curse, is there is no prescribed way.

The developers can pull items in the to-do column and put them into the in-progress column. It is important to limit developers' **Work in Progress or WIP** to usually just one item at a time. In certain cases, they may start something and have to stop and pick something new, but for the most part, we should do one thing at a time until it is complete.

Planning Board

We put items that have just been created on the planning board. We will pull from this planning board when we have a backlog grooming meeting. If you do this, it is best to have a planning board that moves. Once an item has been groomed and estimated, the process of prioritization is next. The Product Owner should guide this process and will help the team decide what can move to the Sprint board with the next Sprint.

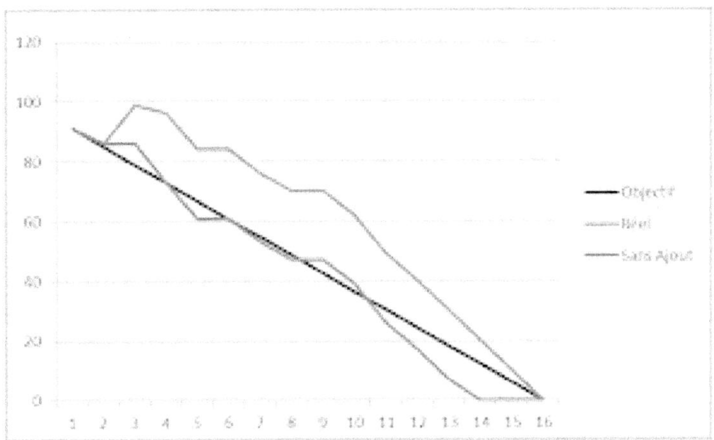

Burndown Chart

Burndown charts show the progress of completing all assigned tasks by the end of the Sprint. This chart can take many shapes as a team progresses through its Sprint workload. If a team is slow to complete anything, this chart will show a horizontal line across it. This may be the case for a team with too large of stories that may need to be broken down further. Burndown charts can warn you early in the Sprint that you may be headed for issues.

If a team starts plowing through its work quickly, you may have an almost vertical line. This can be a case where there is not enough work to complete and the team underestimated what it could do. In this case, the team will have an additional Sprint planning meeting to add more work.

There is an alternative to this called the burnup chart that works the same way, just in reverse. Either way, these charts help you zero in on a date for your next release. These charts also need to be updated frequently, most likely daily. You want to provide up-to-date information to your stakeholders.

About the Author

Tom Henricksen is a problem-solving technology professional. He is a speaker and writer at Code is Easy. Starting from a developer he has worked as a Project Manager, Technical Lead, Scrum Master, and Manager of Software Development.

Tom has helped organizations with agile transformations. He has also coached and trained teams and individuals.

Tom has been an entrepreneur as well. He speaks and writes with a focus on technology roles. Tom was the founder of the Agile Online Summit and DevOps Online Summit where he led a strong online community of over 5,000 people.

Tom has learned how to solve challenging issues in technology and lead technical teams. He can help you develop those skills too!

You can connect with me on:

- 🌐 http://codeiseasy.co
- 🐦 https://x.com/TomHenricksen
- 🔗 https://www.linkedin.com/in/tomhenricksen

Subscribe to my newsletter:

- ✉ https://t.co/NkolrQgXHM